SALAAM

A MUSLIM AMERICAN BOY'S STORY

TRICIA BROWN

PHOTOGRAPHS BY

KEN CARDWELL

HENRY HOLT AND COMPANY • NEW YORK

For peaceful Muslims everywhere,
especially the Ozzie Azam family

The author and photographer gratefully acknowledge:
The Azam family: Ozzie, Sandy, Raheem, Shawn, and Imran; Trevor Gross;
Kristi Doehrer; Emily Gee; Connor Rodriguez; Madison Doehrer;
Alison Stoner; Zubaida Baigum; Jason McCurry; McCurry's Kung-Fu Karate;
Rijn Sahakian; Film Iraq; the Foundation for Iraqi Film Development;
the Al-Bayati family: Mohammed, Boshra, Basma, and, especially, Wisram;
Dr. Metwalli Amer, founder and spiritual leader of SALAM (Sacramento Area
League of Associated Muslims); Cherry Cardwell; Jasmine Cardwell;
Barrett Brown; Andrea Brown; Marjorie Creazzi; Gary Young; Tani and
Jim Edwards; Wendy Snyder; Terry Snyder; and our editor, Reka Simonsen

Henry Holt and Company, LLC
Publishers since 1866
175 Fifth Avenue
New York, New York 10010
www.henryholtchildrensbooks.com

Henry Holt® is a registered trademark of Henry Holt and Company, LLC.
Text copyright © 2006 by Tricia Brown. Photographs copyright © 2006 by Ken Cardwell.
All rights reserved. Distributed in Canada by H. B. Fenn and Company Ltd.

Library of Congress Cataloging-in-Publication Data
Brown, Tricia.   Salaam : a Muslim American boy's story / Tricia Brown;
photographs by Ken Cardwell.—1st ed.
p.   cm.
ISBN-13: 978-0-8050-6538-1 / ISBN-10: 0-8050-6538-5
1. Muslims—United States—Social life and customs—Juvenile literature. 2. Muslims—United States—
Social conditions—Juvenile literature. 3. Muslim boys—United States—Juvenile literature. 4. Muslim families—
United States—Juvenile literature. 5. Islam—United States—Juvenile literature. I. Cardwell, Ken. II. Title.
E184.M88B76 2006   973'.088'297—dc22   2005013147

First Edition—2006 / Designed by Meredith Pratt
Printed in China

1 3 5 7 9 10 8 6 4 2

Imran's story was three years in the making. This delay was due, I believe, to our society's misconceptions about Islam and about Muslims in general. I hope this book will help to clarify who Muslim Americans are and to reduce some of the tensions and misunderstandings that I encountered while working on this book. My hope has always been that the more we know about each other the better friends we can be.

—Tricia Brown

Assalamu

Assalamu alaikum.

That is the Muslim way to say hello. It means

"peace be with you."

My name is Imran, and I am a Muslim American boy.
As a Muslim, I follow Islam, a faith and way of life
based on the practice of the Five Pillars: faith,
prayer, charity, fasting, and pilgrimage to Mecca.

alaikum

I am an American.

I like to play with my
mom and dad in the park,
pet my dog, Tasha, and
celebrate birthdays with
my friends.

I take karate lessons with my older brothers, Raheem and Shawn.

I play games with my cousin, Emily.

And I dream about
becoming a rock
star when I grow up.

I go to school just like you. My best friend, Trevor, and I walk there together every day. This is Mrs. Doehrer, a teacher in our school. We like to tell her jokes.

Trevor and I spend a lot of time at each other's houses.
We talk about everything.

Sometimes we have peanut butter and jelly sandwiches while my mom gets ready to attend service at the mosque.

One time the phone rang. It was someone we didn't know. The person said mean things about our family being Muslim. The call upset her. It makes her sad that some people are mean to our family because of our faith.

Islam has existed for more than thirteen centuries. It is the world's second-largest religion. There are more than one billion Muslims in the world. In the United States, there may be up to ten million of us. We come in all colors and nationalities. And not all Arabs are Muslims: many are Christians or Jews.

My mom wasn't born a Muslim. She became one when she married my dad. At first her parents weren't too happy about her changing her religion. But they felt better when they came to understand that there are many similarities between Muslim beliefs and their own.

It is the custom for Muslim women to cover their heads. The style varies from country to country. In America, wearing the Muslim headscarf, called a *hijab*, is a choice. My mom wears it for holidays and special events. She feels it shows respect for Islam.

My dad thinks a lot of people don't understand what our religion is all about. Islam teaches us to love and respect everyone. We are not supposed to fight or argue. We are not supposed to be mean to anyone.

Trevor asked me if we believe in God. I told him we believe everybody has the same God. We call him Allah, and the Qur'an is our holy book.

We believe the Qur'an was revealed to Muhammad, our most important prophet, 1,400 years ago. Some of the other prophets we believe in are Jesus, Abraham, Moses, and David.

I showed Trevor how we use a compass to point the way to Mecca, which is Islam's holy city. Then we place the prayer rug so that we can face Mecca as we pray.

The times for prayers are calculated according to the phases of the moon. We check a lunar calendar for our prayer times and the times of our holidays.

Mecca is in Saudi Arabia. All Muslims hope to go there at least once in their lifetime. This pilgrimage is called *hajj*. My father shows us a map of Saudi Arabia on the computer. He plans for us to go to Mecca for *hajj* one day.

I told Trevor that another part of being a Muslim is giving to others. What I like best is that the people who receive the charity, or *zakat*, do not know who gave it to them. This year my mom baked sixty dozen cookies to send to the American soldiers overseas. *Zakat* can be given anytime, but it is usually done during Ramadan.

Ramadan is our most important holiday. It takes place during the ninth month of our lunar calendar. During this month, people don't eat from dawn to sunset. This is called fasting. Children are excused from fasting, but I still have to get up with my family before the sun rises. Oh, it is so early! I fall asleep at the table.

Then, after the sun sets, we break the fast and sit down for *iftar*. We never eat pork, and grown-ups don't ever drink alcohol. The *iftar* meal always begins with everyone eating a date.

After Ramadan ends, we celebrate the ending of the fast. This is called Eid al-Fitr. We dress up to go to the mosque where we pray. Ramadan is more than just a month of fasting. It is a time for Muslims to look into themselves and clear up any misunderstandings or problems there may be with other people. It is a time for Muslims to say they are sorry to anyone they have hurt, and a time to forgive anyone who has hurt them.

The Muslims who have come to America, like my dad, are seeking a better life. I look at the picture of my grandmother. She sold all her jewelry so that my dad could come to America. He arrived here with seven hundred dollars in his pocket. He is proud to be an American citizen and is loyal to this country and its laws.

Some people don't understand our beliefs. Maybe when they come to know us better, they will like us, the way our friends and neighbors do. The people who know us respect our differences, and in their hearts they know that we are just like them.

GLOSSARY

Allah (AAH-lah)
God.

Assalamu alaikum
(as-sah-LA-moo ah-LAY-kum)
A greeting meaning "peace be with you."

Eid al-Fitr (EED al-fit-r)
The holiday following Ramadan that
celebrates the end of the month of fasting. Sometimes it is written Eid ul-Fitr.

Hijab (HE-zhaab)
Scarf or veil that a Muslim woman
uses to cover her head.

Hajj (hahj)
Name of the pilgrimage to Mecca.

Iftar (if-TAAR)
The meal at the end of the fasting day
during Ramadan. It takes place at sundown, and everyone present begins by
eating a date.

Mecca (MEH-kah)
The Muslim holy city in Saudi Arabia.
Muslims try to make a pilgrimage there
at least once in their lives.

Mosque (mossk)
The place where Muslims go
to worship.

Qur'an (koh-RAHN)
The holy book of Islam. Muslims
believe that Allah revealed the Qur'an
to the Prophet Muhammad more than
1,400 years ago. It is also spelled Quran
or Koran.

Ramadan (RAHM-ah-dahn)
The ninth month on the lunar calendar.
It is the holy month of fasting for
Muslims.

Salaam (sah-LAHM)
Peace.

Wa alaikum assalam
(wah ah-LAY-kum as-sah-LAHM)
The reply to the Muslim greeting
assalamu alaikum. It means
"And peace with you."

Zakat (zah-KAHT)
Money or goods given to those in
need, usually during the month of
Ramadan.

THE FIVE PILLARS OF ISLAM

For Muslims, the practice of their religion is
a way of life as well. There are five essential
"pillars" of Islam, which every
good Muslim follows:

Shahada. Faith.
A Muslim believes there is one God, Allah.

Salat. Prayer.
Five times a day, Muslims pray to Allah. They look
on the lunar calendar for the times. They use a
prayer rug and a compass that shows
the way to Mecca.

Zakat. Charity.
Muslims give money or goods to those in need.

Sawm. Fasting.
During the month of Ramadan, all adult Muslims
fast. They do not eat or drink anything from
dawn to sundown.

Hajj. Pilgrimage.
Every Muslim should travel to Mecca at least
once in his or her lifetime.

"God does not look at your appearance or your possessions, but He looks at your heart and the things you do."

—Prophet Muhammad